Created By God
By Dr. Mavis Morisseau

Copyright © 2021 by Dr. Mavis Morisseau

All rights reserved. No part of this book may be reproduced in any form or by any electronic or mechanical means, including information storage and retrieval systems, without permission in writing from the publisher or author, except by reviewer or presenter, who may quote brief passages in a review or presentation.

Illustrated by Tonya Monica Mills

Printed in the United States of America
www.sulatoo.com/publishing
ISBN-13:978-1-7358398-9-9 H-cover
ISBN-13:978-1-7365717-0-5 S-cover
ISBN-13:978-1-7365717-1-2 eBook
Children - Religious

Published by
Sula Too Publishing
www.sulatoo.com/publishing

Pastor Mavis Morisseau, an influencer, visionary, motivational speaker, anointed teacher of the word of God was born in San Antonio, Texas. She is the daughter of Wilma Lee Hicks and John Potter. She was stationed in Clovis, New Mexico, and Okinawa, Japan through the military armed forces. She is the proud mother of six daughters and one son. Pastor Mavis has been fulfilling the role of Pastor for the past eight years and has been in ministry for over 20+ years.

Pastor Mavis' initiatives include, educating and training young girls and women. She received her Masters of Creative Movement from Columbia College in Chicago. Her ministry is dedicated to saving souls and spiritual development through prayer and discipleship. Pastor Mavis is an activist for the disadvantaged, spiritually bound, and brokenhearted. Her in-depth teaching includes such topics as, Revelation on Dance Theology, Worship in the Arts, Liturgical Worship, Building Powerful Leaders, operating in the Prophetic, and Establishing Cross-cultural Ministries. She trains and develops leaders of various denominations and ethnic backgrounds. This allows her to effectively mentor spirit-filled persons across the nation to express their artistic ministry in a disciplined and excellent manner.

Pastor Mavis is the Founder of True Worship Prophetic Kingdom Ministry, a church with and without walls. She works side by side with her assistant, Pastor Stephanie Harley to encourage, empower, educate, equip, and edify the body of Christ. Also, Pastor Mavis has worked faithfully with Reach Out to Military Ministry under the leadership of LTC, USAF, Ret. Donna Davis.

Pastor Mavis received an Honorary Doctor of Divinity degree from Eastern Theological Seminary in Lynchburg, Virginia. She is also a member of the Chaplain Ministry Outreach in St. Petersburg, Florida. In October of 2020, Pastor Mavis became a Certified Mental Health Coach where she works with individuals with mental and behavioral health disorders.

As an author, Pastor Mavis gave birth to several books entitled, "Broken, but Not Destroyed," "A Change of Heart, Mind, & Direction", "See yourself the way God sees you", and "Created by God so we must be special!" which is her first children's book.

As a result of her faith and obedience, Pastor Mavis heard from Yeshua Hamashiach in June of 2020 to add "Kingdom" to the ministry's name. The ministry is now operating as True Worship Prophetic Kingdom Ministry (www.twpkministry.com) and continues to unify and reveal the love of Yeshua.

Every day, Pastor Mavis purpose to be better than yesterday and promises to live Yeshua on the inside. Pastor Mavis walks close to Him and close enough to hear God Breathe! Yeshua reigns!

Created by God

Dedicated to God's masterpiece and made in His image

Saraiyah, Iyima, Cheyenne, TaYon, De'jah, Alana, Audrey, Amina, Paityn, Lailah, Micah, Jaiden, Christopher, Aunt Mylan, and Aunt Samenta

~ Love MeMaw

Welcome to **GOD's** creativity in this children's book, it is inspired by **GOD** to impact my family and yours, you will see scriptures come to life and the glory of the Lord through the messages. Children will be able to see themselves, smile and laugh through love, encouragement and beautiful colors, so sit back and enjoy reading to your children, grandchildren, nieces, nephews or community. For the presence of **GOD's** love will be fulfilled and His light will radiate all through these pages. **GOD's** love is my source and my supply, and in His goodness and mercy towards us, I am honored to leave this legacy for all generations to come.

Acts 17:28, Psalm 16:11

Saraiyah

GOD gave Saraiyah her beautiful eyes, so that she could see all the amazing things from the big blue skies.

Like the eagles, and birds that soar, you are the diamond that shines brighter than anything in this world that roars. You are fearfully and wonderfully made, and I see you strong and tall marching in that kingdom parade. Saraiyah you have been chosen for Greatness, as you kneel at His throne, so never let your peers out there treat you wrong.

Saraiyah you are the Deborah's and Jael's in GOD's Holy word, and soon all over the world your voice will be heard.

You may be the future scientist or maybe an astronaut, but family don't forget about her graduation one day full of what-me-knots. Basketball, soccer, running track, or even painting just might be your scholarship in a HBCU ranking. Hugs and kisses will always come your way, remember to embrace them all in your own very special way. Mimi loves you. Mommy loves you too but never ever forget the GOD who made you!

Ecclesiastes 11:7

Mimi loves you beautiful granddaughter

Iyima

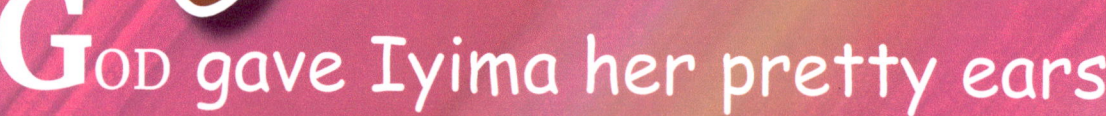

God gave Iyima her pretty ears

So that she could hear all the many sounds both far and near;

Like the blue robin bird looking for her nest flying up and down the skies missing all the rest. The chirping sound is so very sweet and I know Iyima would love to have this bird for keeps.

She also has a monkey name George, that she lays down to sleep.

I know for sure he is definitely for keeps. Her favorite cartoons are boss baby and baby shark. Let's not forget about Noah's Ark.

Mommy gives her big hugs and kisses all the time and she makes sure to keep Iyima on her mind. It's a new day for fun in the sun, this beautiful family loves the beat of the drum.

Saraiyah keeps her laughing and playing all the time, but Iyima knows when it's her nap time.
Proverbs 15:31

Mimi loves you beautiful granddaughter

Cheyenne

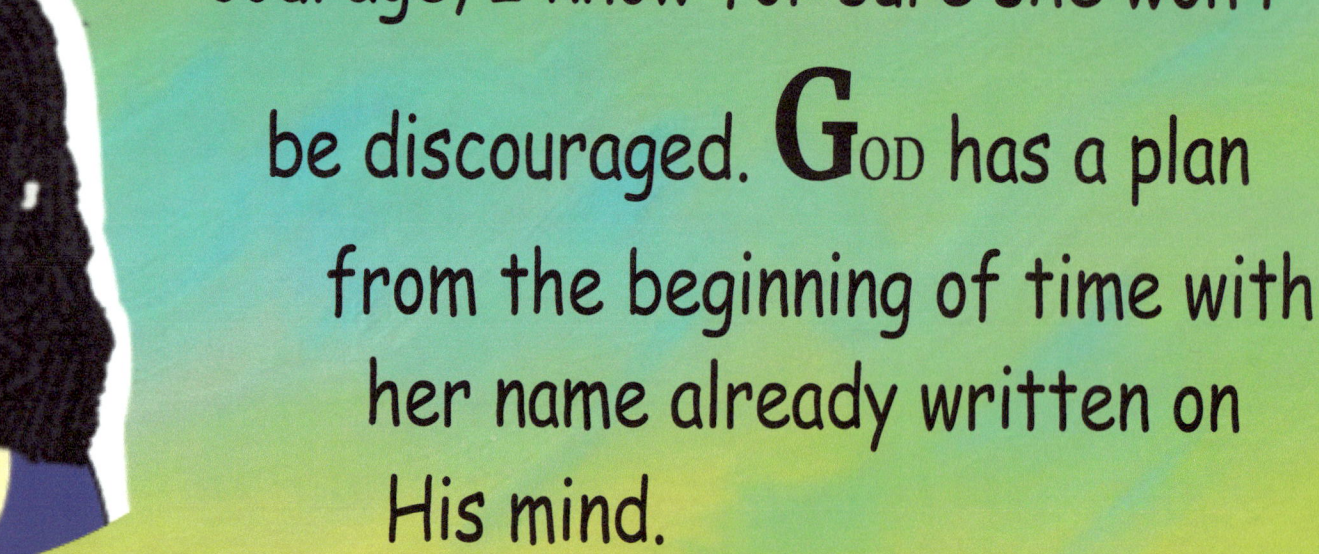

God gave Cheyenne her brilliant mind so she could be creative all the time. Since she is sitting on the shoulders of greatness and courage, I know for sure she won't be discouraged. God has a plan from the beginning of time with her name already written on His mind.

She is the beautiful big sister to God's masterpiece, and He makes no mistakes with keeping their peace.

She loves playing video games, even riding her bike, as long as it's not too dark or late at night. Flying a kite is fun too, but she much rather go to Kalamazoo.

Ephesians 2:10

Memaw loves you beautiful

TaYon

God gave TaYon her beautiful hair so she could feel the breeze from the air. She likes jumping rope, running, and climbing big trees, or playing freeze tag and maybe looking for honeybees.

She is a ray of sunshine all day long, her mommy and daddy shows her just how much she belongs.

G OD kisses her on her forehead each and every day to remind her He is never too far away. Roses are red and violets are blue,

TaYon is so precious, and G OD said so too.

Numbers 6:25

Memaw loves you beautiful one

De'jah

God gave De'jah her pretty hands, and mommy loves watching her crawl and stand. She loves hugs and kisses throughout the day, even when it's time for her to play, her blocks are fun and colorful too, but she enjoys the orange birds at the North Carolina zoo.

She is bright like the sun with a twinkle in her eyes. I know mommy and daddy also loves looking into her big beautiful brown eyes.

Habakkuk 3:4

Memaw loves you so much

Alana

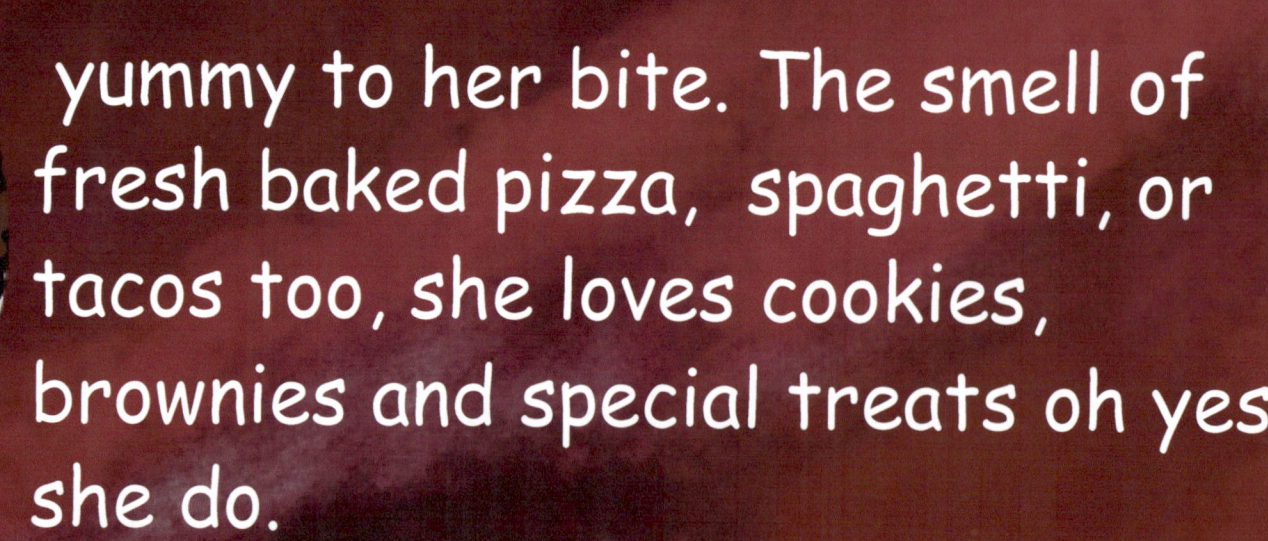

God gave Alana her gorgeous nose so that she could smell that pretty pink rose. Like sugar, coated rainbow chunks and marshmallow delights or caramel candy popcorn which is yummy to her bite. The smell of fresh baked pizza, spaghetti, or tacos too, she loves cookies, brownies and special treats oh yes she do.

Alana really enjoys her arts and crafts, so she and mommy can make tall and beautiful giraffes. Her friends like coming over to play, but she likes asking them to stay.

When mommy or daddy say it's time to go, Alana says no, no, no.

2 Corinthians 2:15

Memaw loves you a million trillion!

Audrey

God gave Audrey her million-dollar smile, so she can be the light of the world, even to the wild. Her pretty dimple is a joy to see, just as sweet as a cup of peach iced tea. She loves to laugh and sing Twinkle Twinkle Little Star, on a piano that's way too far.

Make some cupcakes and she is pleased, long enough to say may I have some more please.

She is so adorable and loving as can be, and Memaw never stop saying, please don't forget about me.

God touches her heart each and every day, especially when she kisses Amina while she plays.

God loves her so much, even in His very special touch.

Proverbs 15:13

Memaw loves you a hundred thousand

Amina

God gave Amina her beautiful feet so she could dance, dance, dance to every single beat! And He blessed her with those soft fat cheeks.

She reaches for Mommy all day long, just to realize she is so very strong. Nursery rhymes are wonderful to hear, if you create them from your own heart deep down with cheer.

Amina is a student in Melamom's class. And 'Oh Boy!' she is learning sooooooo fast! She knows her letters and colors already and by next year she will be strong and steady.

She is a bundle of joy to everyone she meets, and they all remember how much she loves to eat.

Proverbs 4:26-27

Memaw loves you precious one

Paityn

God gave Paityn her loving heart so she could feel the blessings right from the start. She is loving, polite, and sweet. But most of all she will keep her sister Lailah on her feet.

She loves tumbling, flipping and running all day long. And she will let you know that she is beautiful and very strong. Make-up is fun and pretty as can be, but she loves her nails done so gracefully.

They have two dogs they love so much, but mommy and daddy say it's just too much.

Alright girls its story time, and they are both ready for bedtime. Goodnight sleep tight and remember you are truly

Gᴏᴅ's awesome delight.

Matthew 22:37

Memaw loves you so much

Lailah

GOD gave Lailah her special gifts like writing, coloring, and tumbling too and she gives you big hugs if you want her too. She makes her own tent for family to come and play, before she commands everyone to stay, she has a twin sister named Paityn who loves her dearly, I promise you GOD made them both cheerfully.

She loves to eat and have extra treats, don't be surprised if she gives it all to every one she meets.

She enjoys seeing lightning bugs outside at night, but oh my gosh she hopes they don't bite. She just might say,
Go away! Go away!
I just don't want to play!

Philippians 4:13

Memaw loves you a whole bunch

Micah

God gave Micah his awesome strength not only to recognize his confidence, but like Samson in the Word, he is strong, handsome and smart.

Like Noah who made God's awesome great ark. His future is purposed, promised and steady.

When God says it's time, he will be ready. Heaven is his open door, as he looks upon the poor.

One day GOD will say absolutely no more. Keep praying for our future generations to come, and I promise you one day GOD will say Well Done!

It's a sunny day with bright sunshine for trucks and cars and boats and planes, even watching him ride on his choo choo train.

It's time for bed, with big kisses and hugs from both Mommy and Daddy with lots of love.

2 Corinthians 12:8-10

Memaw loves you so much

Jaiden

God gave Jaiden his amazing legs, so he could run relays and pull those sleighs. He plays basketball and football all the time, and the angels watch over him and say he's mine. He loves to laugh and play with his brother, and he never ever forgets about his mother.

His daddy, auntie and grandma watch him climb those trees, but G<small>OD</small> gives him the love to pray on his knees.

Hebrews 12:1

Memaw loves you so much

Christopher

God gave Christopher his rosy cheeks and that big smile gets him all the sweets. His tubby tummy is so fat, that he can't hold on like his little friend Jack.
I could tickle tickle him in the Tub and Jaiden would say, rubba dub dub.

He cries when you take his toys, and his brother will say, Chris stop that noise. Now it's time to play peek a boo, so you can stop all that boo hoo hoo.

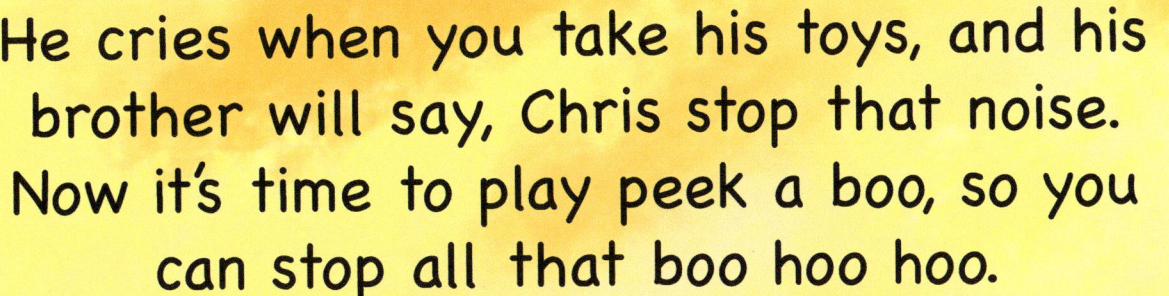

Psalm 2:4

Memaw loves you so much

Aunt Mylan

Gᴏᴅ gave Aunt Mylan a new beginning, knowing
she would be the one always winning.
She is full of love, joy, and peace;
because she knows the creator who she must keep.
She loves her nieces, nephews and cousins too, and that is just to name a few.

God gave her His gift of poetry and song, so that she could write almost all day long. Whether trial or tribulation she will make it through because God made her a prolific writer and great leader too.

Luke 5:36-38, 2 Corinthians 5:17

Mommy loves you so very much

Auntie Samenta

GOD gave Auntie Samenta her servant's heart, so she could love and care for people from the start. She is friendly, kind and full of compassion, and it doesn't matter if they don't dress in the latest fashion.

She loves to cook and make special treats and give to her community all who love to eat.

She is the beautiful Ebony of GOD's creation, and has love ones from the Haitian nation. Her sisters and brother love her dearly, but Mylan truly holds her close, sincerely.

You are amazing, awesome and smart, but guess what daughter, I knew that from the very start.

Galatians 5:13

Mommy loves you so very much

MeMaw

God gave Memaw all eleven of my grandchildren, and blessed me with my beautiful children, so He would get all the glory and praise. I am grateful to leave a legacy of love, joy, and forgiveness, but hugs and kisses all the days of their lives is the best gift God could grant me. I realize now, with all the extra children, God had a plan all along. I just didn't know it would take this long.

God is not moved by space or time, now I know we were all on His mind. Wisdom, Knowledge, and Understanding is who He is.

It's not about me, but His will. He may not come when I want, but He is always on time. He is Sovereign. His name is Yahweh, and I belong to Him.

I love my God with all of me and He chose me as the one who would love others endlessly.

Psalm 103:19

The Lord's Prayer

Our Father who art in Heaven
hallowed be they name.
Thy kingdom come, thy will be done,
on earth as it is in Heaven.
Give us this day our daily bread
and forgive us our trespasses,
as we forgive those who trespass against us.
Lead us not into temptation
but deliver us from evil.
For thine is the kingdom, the power
and the glory, forever and ever.

Amen

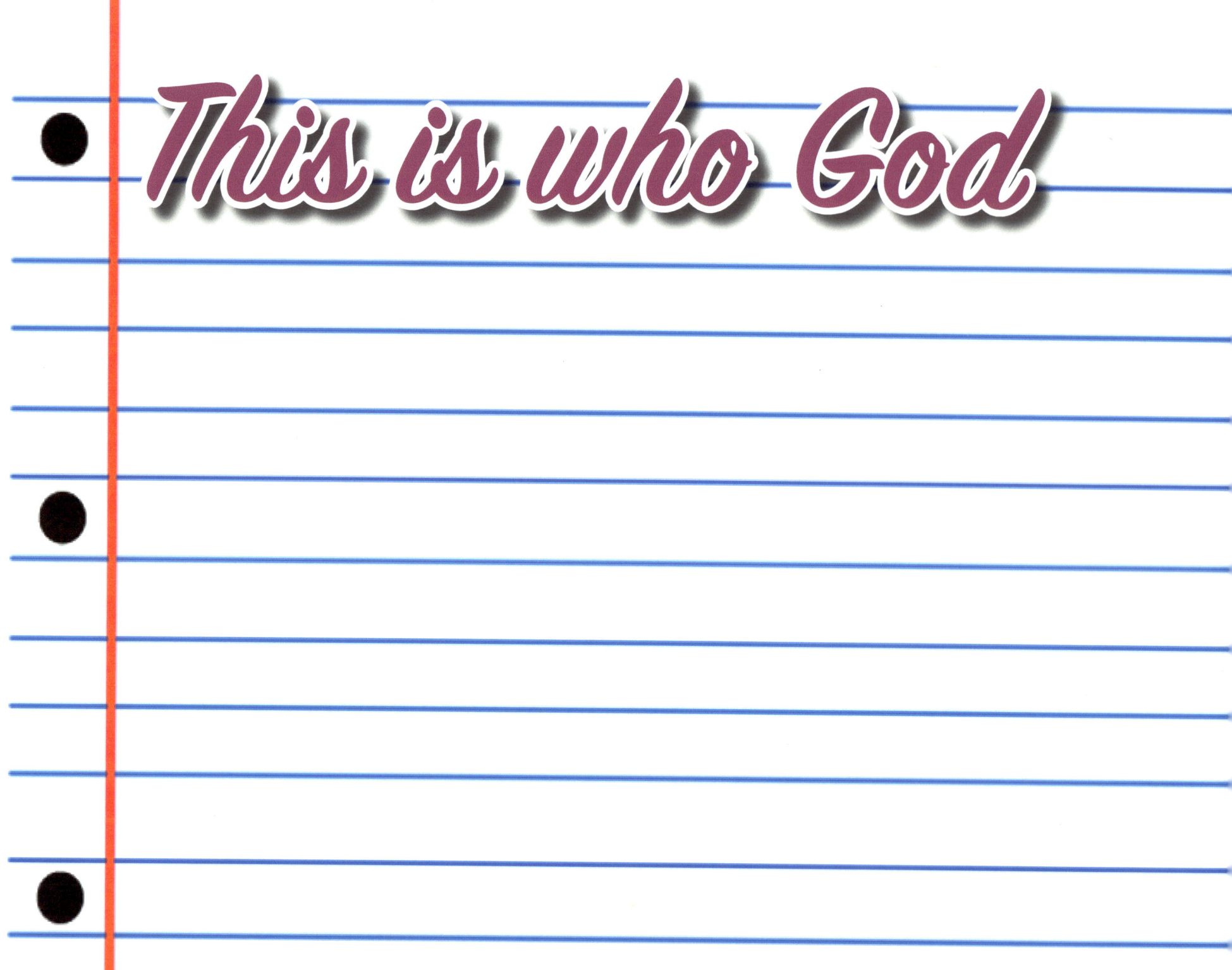
This is who God

created me to be...

> Take a Pen! Take a Pencil and write down **EVERYTHING** **I am** meant to be!

from your heart

Draw a comic from

your imagination

Your favorite words

Your favorite ideas

God gave me this vision to write a children's book and dedicate it to my children and grandchildren. I am so very proud of my family, it's so beautiful serving the Lord, and being the best person, I could ever become according to my Father's Word. As a woman of integrity and Godly character, I have learned so many valuable lessons. Lord thank you for continuing to lead, guide and strengthen me in all my ways, I am so grateful to be chosen by you to write these messages to my babies and others whose lives I am able to impact. It's a new season, new day and fresh anointing. It's a season of power and authority, I pray all who read this book and share with others, that the Lord God Almighty will continue to bless all the beautiful fathers and mothers. May His Word richly dwell with you and keep you wrapped in His arms. May His face shine upon you and keep you in perfect peace in Yeshua's Name. 　　　　　　　　　　　　　　　Amen.

Ms Ladii Rollins
  Saraiyah Rollins
  Iyima Rollins

Chris & Jonae Scott
  Micah Rollins Scott

Joseph & Nyjah Rollins
  Paityn Rollins
  Lailah Rollins

Auntie Mylan Morisseau

Deven & Chavon Harris
  Cheyenne Stroud
  TaYon Stroud
  DeJah Harris

Andre & Ashonta Johnson
  Alana Johnson
  Audrey Johnson
  Amina Johnson

Nakia Hanley
  Jaiden Bryant
  Christopher Crowe, Jr.

Auntie Samenta Morisseau

May His Word richly

To all 11 of my grandchildren and my two daughters,

dwell with you...

I love, love, love you ALL so very much!!

www.ingramcontent.com/pod-product-compliance
Lightning Source LLC
Chambersburg PA
CBHW041108210426

43209CB00063BA/1852